CATHERINE PHIL MacCARTHY wa
and educated at University Coll
Dublin and Central School of Speech and Drama, London.
Joint winner of the Poetry Ireland/Co-operation North Sense
of Place competition in 1991, a selection of her work was
published in *How High the Moon*. Her first collection, *This Hour
of the Tide*, was published by Salmon Poetry in 1994, and her
second, *The Blue Globe*, by Blackstaff Press in 1998. She was
writer in residence for the City of Dublin in 1994, for
University College Dublin in 2002, and editor of *Poetry Ireland
Review* in 1998. Her first novel, *One Room an Everywhere*, was
published by Blackstaff Press in 2003.

PRAISE FOR CATHERINE PHIL MacCARTHY

'quirky and emotional ... MacCarthy has the insight, the grace and the humour to realise that it is these apparently small things which for the most part, and for most people, prove to be the very biggest episodes of our lives.'

JO RODGERS, *Irish Post*

'executed with skilful economy and a painterly deftness ... these poems quietly convey a powerful sense of the value of experience'

CAITRÍONA O'REILLY, *Irish Times*

'Now and then, one comes upon a collection whose maturity and sense of poetic certainty give one fresh hope for an Irish poetry scene ... MacCarthy's poems have a worked edge, a sureness of tone and a command of language ... Reading her work ... one grows envious of the neat, taut tensions of some poems and the lucid, dramatic balance of others.'

FRED JOHNSTON, *Sunday Tribune*

'This is not just a book I'm reading, it's one I'll return to. The poems are fresh, definite snapshots of very elusive feelings ... the work of a very gifted, very interesting and new Irish poet.'

EAVAN BOLAND, *Irish Times*

suntrap

catherine phil maccarthy

April 1 2007 Dublin,

For Catherine

In admiration & friendship

Catherine Phil MacCarthy

BLACKSTAFF
PRESS
BELFAST

First published in 2007 by
Blackstaff Press
4c Heron Wharf, Sydenham Business Park
Belfast BT3 9LE
with the assistance of
The Arts Council of Northern Ireland

© Catherine Phil MacCarthy, 2007

COVER IMAGE: *Automatic Shift* (1969)
by Allen Jones, b.1937
© Allen Jones 2006
Collection: Ulster Museum, Belfast
Photograph reproduced with the kind permission of the
Trustees of the National Museums Northern Ireland

Typeset by Carole Lynch, County Sligo, Ireland
Printed in England by Cromwell Press

A CIP catalogue record for this book is available
from the British Library

ISBN 978-0-85640-801-4
www.blackstaffpress.com

for Rachel,
David and Justin

The dream of my life
Is to lie down by a slow river
And stare at the light in the trees –
To learn something by being nothing
A little while but the rich
Lens of attention.

MARY OLIVER
from 'Entering the Kingdom',
New and Selected Poems (1992)

When we are confronted by an emotional difficulty or danger, there are three things we can do. We can pretend that *we* are not there, i.e. we can become feeble-minded or ill; we can pretend that *it* isn't there, i.e. we can daydream; or we can look at it carefully and try to understand it, understand the mechanism of the trap. Art is a combination of these last two; there is an element of escape in it, and an element of science, which only differs from what we generally call by that name, in that its subject is a different order of data.

W.H. AUDEN
from 'Poetry, Poets, and Taste',
The English Auden (1977)

CONTENTS

SURFACING

after Eugenio Montale

Bright mornings,
when the blue is magic that doesn't fool,
growing immense with life,
swollen river with no banks, no limit,
flows forever,
and stays – eternally.

Now there are sounds on the road,
the crack in the window,
the stone that falls
on the mirror of the lake and ripples it.
And the calling of the boys
and the fluent chitchat of sparrows
flitting between the eaves
are trellises of gold
on a vivid deep of cobalt,
ephemeral . . .

Here, and lost in the net of echoes,
in the breath of hoar
that falls on the thinned trees
and draws from them a murmur
of restless shore,
you could almost, and it shakes you,
engrossed heart, dissolve
and beat no more! But always when you long for this
you beat stronger, like
a clock striking in a hotel bedroom
at the first tremor of dawn.

1

And you feel then,
even if they say again that you may
stop halfway, or on the high seas,
that there's no rest for us,
only the road, more road,

and always the journey to begin again.

THE FREEDOM OF THE CITY

He slips out the back gate
with a young woman –
fair hair, pouting lips
and long ethnic skirts –

an old man with keys in his hand,
his bald head turned
to check the lie of the land,
that one backward glance

cautious as the bushy-tailed
red fox whose eyes met mine
in our garden after rain
one November afternoon

in a deluge of green
between leaf-fall and sunshine,
before he turned to light again
high on the boundary wall.

ORIGINS

Summers the pump ran dry,
the water level in the stone well

never changed, each time
the silvery upturned bucket

dropped ten feet or more,
a damp air of moss and lichen,

the rim plumbed clear stillness,
struck one staccato volley.

When the handle disappeared
the bucket filled and sank,

the rope chafed on my hands,
stretched taut, found depth,

weight keeled on my palm.
I raised arm over arm,

fingers weaving a tight plait –
to rein the pendulum swing

against rock, the crash
and slop into vacant pitch,

as the rope grew short
and my spine sore –

one last hoist to the curb,
aching to be grown,

rise a young woman
in layers of fluent chiffon,

clear of the ground
brimming onto land,

bright and round
as the moon.

PHYSICIAN

The stitches were spindly and black,
insect legs down the ridge of my nose,
thirteen exquisite bows.
They smelt of death and surgical spirit,
tiny fissures of dried blood.

Where had my doctor learnt to sew?
At nine my love was embroidery.
Coiled skeins of silk that gleamed
and hung like miniature ponytails.
Stem, chain, herring-bone,

cross, satin. Palm-green leaves,
a tiny oasis of tenderness
on the jute cushion cover at home.
We were eye to eye and so close.
The lines on my hands told

rough work on the farm.
His fingers were pink and manicured
when he pressed the bone
as if to measure something.
Mother said I was lucky,

some doctors were only butchers.
The cut had knit invisibly.
He and I had something in common.
Only one of us knew. Perfect
stitching marked us both.

SUNTRAP

After tea, in the front yard the old man
asks for my hand, the hand of a child.
He wants to show me a magnifying glass,
the closest thing he has to a toy,

and I'm bored, though my palm under it
is pink, fantastic. Now he dips
the silvery rim as if he's fishing air
to trap the sun on newspaper, angling it

closer so it smoulders and takes fire,
and I learn for the first time how to burn.

TALKING TO GOD
IN A PROTESTANT CHURCH

We stole inside once, school bags dropped
by the baptismal font. Stone walls,
flag floor, no coloured mosaic
in symmetries of lambs or doves

or paradise lost, no incense smells,
statues of the saints or
Virgin Mary in a blue robe
standing on the globe,

one bare foot on a snake's head,
no Stations of the Cross,
but crests to major or colonel
who died in Gallipoli or Dunkirk.

Pews with high wooden backs,
velvet cushions for knees,
brass names adorning each row.
We climbed in at *Lady Jane Harrington*,

married twice – 'God didn't mind,'
Father said, 'they had different rules
and tried their best.' We'd seen her
on the horse. Our pulses raced

as we took a seat and bowed our heads
wondering which husband came to church,
beyond the pulpit found instead
faded regimental flags,

a vase of dried grass,
radiant daylight streaming in
through clear glass,
the savage yearning of our hearts.

NORTH AND SOUTH

You asked me to pray for you at the wedding
in the First Presbyterian Church
in Ballybay – built from stone in 1640
with plaques on the wall
dedicated to the fallen in 1914 –
and we danced so close
to the border,
God was listening.

SEEDS

Giant, freckled,
my father's hands
scatter grain, palms
cast from a jute sack
this way and that as if
he's performing a rite.
And what I wonder about is
how he measures out
the ground and how he knows
how thick and fast to plant
as he paces forward
and where exactly it lands.
The Bible warns against stones.
What about the birds
already having a feast
as they flock and lift,
treating our harrowed space
as if it were Christmas?

He's unconcerned about stones
and it's important to cater
for the birds. They'll soon
have enough. As for the seeds,
I watch them sprout
delicate ribby greens
against the rainy earth
and rise over months to a deep
aquamarine that glistens
in runnels under the breeze.

Avid to catch the split
second the colours change,
I play hide-and-seek
in an emerald smock,
vanish and appear,
eye to eye with ripening grain
stilled by a tide
shifting the field,
and close my eyes to listen
as the harvest turns golden.

SPARROW THIEVES

It put the cat among the pigeons –
though my fears were black and white –
that day the magpies surrounded the cat,
a sparrow in his mouth,

stealing through grass. Raucous and harsh,
they hovered and clacked, cornering him
between the Moroccan broom and the kitchen,
from where I saw him stop dead

in his tracks as one flew down
from gable to branch, another from
washing-line to land, a third dive-bombed.
He dropped the bird, who just lay

flailing her squashed wing onto blades
of grass, the heart still pumping as he
belly-dragged back – and a fourth swooped down
to snatch into the air the stolen catch.

OUT OF TOUCH

You switched on the light
but the small reception room stayed

dark. We stood awkward as cats
at such instant contact. It gets worse.

Last night I closed my eyes
in a room full of friends talking

to find us slow dancing
in luxurious darkness,

your palm to the small of my back,
our hands loosely clasped,

my brow so close to your lips
we are guided by your breath.

Already, know what I miss?
Under the stars, your goodnight kiss.

PAOLO AND FRANCESCA

after Rodin

They sit there ignoring us,
engrossed in a first kiss,
so wrapped up
in themselves
that we behold them,

nonplussed.
The book in his hand
just slipped to the ground,
the page he was reading,
of Guinevere and Lancelot,

open face down.
She has taken to heart
his medieval romance,
wrung by a kiss,
hungry for the taste

of his mouth,
the soft play of his lips.
Outside their window
is birdsong and sunshine,
red roofs, the Adriatic

glittering.
She doesn't know yet
that love will bring them,
light on the wind,
true selves,

one death,
sweeping in like the sea
they played in as children,
bodies innocent
of all suffering.

THE FIRST ROD:
MACKEREL AT INIS OÍRR

Cast the line off the pier,
summer nights
into black stillness,
read the dusk blind,
Atlantic waters at full tide.
Wrist so deft and light
arching the throw
high and wide now,
all six flies kiss
the slick surface like stars
shooting without trace

where a shoal
in its own sweet hour
clots and ripples a current
to the hands, charged
at the least quiver
to reel in the bowed line
amid whoops and cries,
at pains to land
the weight of this prize,
wriggling and twitching
with silvery light.

ISLAND OF MIRACLES

Forty degrees. Not a soul on the beach.
I began to dream of rain
as we lay in our shuttered room,
blood growing thin,

of standing in a field
drenched to the skin, tongue out
drinking as it poured down,
of falling to my knees before the heavens.

We sped north and east,
the hot wind from Africa burning our heels,
rose with the road, with our fear,
the breath of an angry god,

through mountains above a ravine
round Kera Pass,
you could no longer steer
and our bike was a trembling reed.

I turned my face from the precipice
as you steadied the wheel
in that land of the mother goddess,
and drove at full throttle.

I could feel our lives in our hands,
then mercy of the elements
as we flew to the plain
of a thousand springs

where the gale ceased
by the cave of baby Zeus,
and we glimpsed the shadow
of an eagle floating downstream.

CAMPING IN MESQUIER

We glimpsed ocean first cycling past
sunlit marshes and stone cottages,
unpacked at a site near the coast

in that quickening hour, sunset
to dark. Home was a book,
a grove of pines, an isthmus

encircled in salt wind,
inflamed with bites of *moustiques*.
Nights we drank in resinous dusk,

cocooned by squabbles
of Breton children, a pair of fireflies
dancing in the glow of kerosene.

TORNADO

A charcoal funnel – like smoke, spiralling from a blanched sky,
we as a young couple saw
in the distance spin

towards land across the bay before we left the surf
at Matala, along the dunes,
sand cutting our eyes –

must have followed us here, as you called me
to watch on TV in our sitting room,
the eye of the storm

on its path towards land, hanging from sky
to ground, the wild sea,
wrecked house,

a lone man in rain-gear, up to his knees in waves,
shovelling pebble-stones
to hold a breakwater,

and coming back to me, how you
huddled on our things,
tent blown down,

and sand-grains under our eyelids
made us
blind.

WISHING TREE IN CYPRUS

Along the slope of a high road near the sea
past the scent of orange groves
and the Bath of Aphrodite
stands the wishing tree,

a young oak against the blue sky,
spread branches draped with white muslin
rags – a severed country –
littered with secret pleas,

flown beyond checkpoints, barbed wire,
borders, and riding
the summer breeze,
where larks dip

and soar in the singing air,
fields of gorse blossom
to the shore and the road meanders
eastward like a winding stair.

FUGIT AMOR

At the Musée Rodin I looked for us
among the lovers. We were never that
fierce, a couple twinned in flight,
white marble bodies all delicate curve

back to back lying across air. And yet.
How those arms reach over his head,
seize her shoulder, her breast,
how she strains beyond his hands

free and fleet as a bird. They were
once a world lost, abandoned flesh,
and in that searing rush how could they
not fall apart? Look at mouths

averted, bodies caught in space.
He is cast over her, facing the heavens,
she is facing earth. Stretched
on that rack, desire holds them

still, governs her tongue, consumes
him. Here, see how love fares
beyond death, tender as hell,
transports like doves' wings.

NOT SLEEPING TOGETHER

My legs, bare and lithe, straddle your hips,
in the slowly swaying dark
my head on your shoulder is light.

After all the excitement of the last days,
lover-boy, here's the surprise:
I am suddenly back in time.

Against your strength my bones grow soft,
I could be eight or nine.
This is how we are as night comes down:

you still standing as darkness encroaches
and I, falling deep and fast, my arms wrapped
tight around the world.

FRESH TRACKS

. . . a high place thins your thoughts
                    Jan Owen

Each dawn above the waking
crunch of skiers on the bridge,
armed and ready for the mountain,
what I sensed

in our sweet hollow (that high dry note
giving us a key for the whole day)
was the rising sun
full on that ridge,

so when we looked at the sky first thing
that peak rose sheer and pink
out of blue infinity,
a vision from a Japanese print,

belonging more to heaven than earth.
Mornings we ascended
over snowy roofs and laden trees,
climbing crisscross, lift after lift,

our bodies unhoused and tense,
discovering all over again
that it's by breathing we live
and with each breath

we are a little closer to death.
Tipped from the lift onto our skis,
light was shimmering sequins,
atmosphere, celestial.

Above the clouds and drifting
fields, we contemplate
incorporeal peaks, world
as we know it at our feet.

TERRIERS

Baying on the doorstep
like a pack at close quarters,
they entered his dreams.

He spat back and growled
a low bush snarl

as they cornered him,
then mauled the scruff
of his cowering neck,
delicate as antique porcelain,
fierce as lovers, teeth sunk
so deep he moaned

while I hauled them off
by the hair on their pelts,
one in each hand, and he shot
into still undergrowth,

Persian coat fluffed out,
tufts of fur flaring
onto red and black mosaic,
long weathered, discoloured.

It made me wonder about
their eagerness to
tear him open
when he was least expecting –

in fact, languidly waking,
a model of Zen recreation,
that gaze of insouciance,
gracefulness, his essence.

SUANTRAÍ

She wakes up beside him,
a nocturne's spilt notes,
how he's cupped in her arms.

Will he in time forget all this?
That for once he's the lover
who rose at dawn,

Díarmuid on a mountain-side,
her naked body, an unentered pool,
and here they find themselves

content in a silence of breathing
that scent drenched in the song of a bird
at the open window and light

billowing through a soft fall of rain
and dare not utter a word
for fear of breaking the spell.

MOTHER TONGUE

English and Irish
words in my dream are
lines of a poem,

guth mumbling
as I wake,
vowels that heal

the sore throat
of language and tongue
into *teanga*.

ANOTHER WOMAN

When he makes love to me
her smiling face I see,
perspiration on her skin,

hair gleaming in sunshine,
hand-printed cotton skirt
falling from the waist in colours

of an aboriginal artwork
to the camel suede of her boots.
Should I tell him there's

another woman in the bed?
Does he already know and turn
a blind eye, that her energy

drives me as I touch him,
and the sobbing tenderness
he draws from me anoints her?

DANCE

Our clothes fade away.
Stripes crisscross our bodies,
glisten head to toe,
colours of the rainbow.

United with such force
we are our primal selves –
each other's body –
skin and bone.

GRÁINNE'S BED

On this grassy mound, my love,
you are meshed in a web of blossom,
pale body entwined with stems,

violets, heartsease, wild roses.
I am summer earth holding you
in a dreaming clasp between my thighs,

taking you inside, time and again,
the deep lair of my being where
your seed sprouts from my blood.

IN THE SMALL HOURS

She overhears you sing downstairs one night
of when your waters broke, how he rose
in the small hours, your pain both dark and light,

he tackled horse and trap by moonlight
and drove straight to town as you passed out.
She overhears you sing downstairs one night

of how the horse's hooves woke the street
and the midwife hurried to your side,
in the small hours, the pain now dark not light.

You prayed to God, pushing for all your might;
boiled water, towels, a knife, they cried.
She overhears you sing downstairs one night.

The head came forth but you were out of sight,
dazed and tired when the cord was cut,
in the small hours, the pain less dark than light.

You slept and slept the sleep of the dead,
in the nurse's arms the child was fed.
She overhears you sing downstairs at night,
in the small hours, your love now dark and light.

EVASIONS

When you reached 'the terrible twos'
I kept an eye out for puppies, kittens,
even hedgehogs peeping from
behind the houses as we rode past

on the bus. Anything to distract you
from rages. 'There's a horsey, see,
by the bushes. Don't you see it?'
As you picked yourself up,

face blotched from screams,
eyes wet, your face relaxed with
'Show me' and we put our heads
together while you sat on my lap

and gazed at the scene.
Now that you're almost ten
and trying on thirteen,
'Cool', 'So?' or 'Crap!'

pepper your vocabulary.
I'm on the look-out for rainbows,
new moons, shooting stars,
something to counter, 'Bitch! I hate you!'

THE BIG FREEZE

The snow has no voice.
　　　Sylvia Plath

She had on her worn coat for milking,
fawn wool scarf tied at her chin,
black kid gloves for mass,
tiny holes patterning the back,

when she went into the boiler house
to fetch the axe

and took my hand as we walked
out the yard past the gate
into broken ground
of the cow-stand, hoof-marks
glazed with doilies of frost.

We might as well have
stumbled through cut glass,
grazing our shins as far as
the drinking trough,
sheeted clear with packed ice,

the Shannon in the news
that morning frozen a mile wide.

Our breaths plumed in the air
as the blade rang solid as rock
against each chip
that flew like smashed flint,
and tiny capillaries in Mother's face
grew livid with effort.

I was hoping for the ice to win,
despite the whitening crater.

WONDERSTRUCK

She watched you tread
the glistening ice
as you advanced
beyond the point.
All her care,
a deafening cry

above white pines,
echoed round the frozen lake,
your name one syllable
flung with love,
faint at your unheeding back.
Cold air pinched your neck.

Eyes splintered with light,
you skipped deep
into warm sunshine.
Ice held like glass
under the sole of your boot,
a solid expanse

sounding a tap
made you want to dance.
The water looked black.
You could see it seep
under the weight of your foot.
You could see bird-tracks,

grass caught in opaque.
You even spotted fish.
That instant you were God
carried towards
the long deep channel
that speedboats race in summer.

One moment you were there
before her eyes,
the next, skinned.
You wanted to shriek *Mother,*
Mother, but your mind was a howl,
Let me out, let me out.

Treading hard against
the weight of dark
to a trap of light
was your instinct to survive.
Under that crystal roof
you were the only clamour.

MUTINY

'Shame! Shame!' The children echo
their granny in consternation
taking the law into her own hands
in a baleful attempt to stop high jinks

with the wooden spoon, while they
played in the hall and raced upstairs,
brazening the scorch of her temper.
'Shame!' they chant back in chorus,

bait her threats to give them a whack,
mimic the tone of severity,
the sound of the word in their mouths
taking wind from her sails like

a curse or some ancient trespass,
that instant cacophony of voices
invoking its power as they wonder at
its sense, the way it halts vocabulary.

DELUGE

They throw Beanie Babies across the fence
and shout their names and call for someone

to throw them back. I sit quiet with a book
pretending not to exist as animals rain,

but they have climbed onto a ledge and spied
a patch of dress through the lattice and red

roses, blooming all round a gap in the hedge.
Already there are lions, elephants, penguins,

and several species of reptile looking sad.
'Here's Amber,' they holler undeterred.

A striped cat lands at my feet. Two pairs
of brown eyes observe. 'Would you like to

keep him?' They smile as I pick up the cat.
Amber is soft, enough to take me off guard.

More Beanies shower the fence. The boys are
yelling and it's time for bed, but from

their incessant voices I can hear
exhaustion flooding the land,

their parents are already drowned
and I understand what Noah in the Ark must

have felt: I am their only chance
and my garden is the last high island left.

BAILIFF

Authority is an old man
with a hat and a big stick,
entering the yard in a temper.

At bedtime, on sight of him,
like sprites small children scatter.
When he calls out a name

she stands her ground by a door
then chases down a corridor
to hide where he can't see her.

Even though it drives him mad
(he has been to the pub),
at the risk of a beating

she is unable to stop
provoking him with glimpses
that say, 'You can't catch me.'

THE AGE OF REASON

Gulliver – shipwrecked
on the way to Van Diemen's Land
and washed ashore – woke,
the little people of Lilliput
crawling up the great edifice of
his leg and onto his chest,

in a fever, half-opened sore eyes
to blinding light, a burning sky –
unable to stir an inch
for the weight of pinned limbs,
hair matted, head

swimming – while they came
and went, tiptoeing
to the ministry of their curiosity,
and he slept and woke
defenceless as they probed

the length and breadth of him.
At the pinch of minute hands
undoing buttons,
even a child aged seven

fathoms – pariah
fed and watered –
how it must stand,

craving above all else
his own kind,
to be mighty and unmanned.

43

PATTERN

I nearly walked into it,
the spider's web hung

in a sunlit clearing
between two trees,

imagined the wreckage
of silk filaments

against my face.
This one glistened intact,

its spun mesh
geometrically perfect –

netting a morning's light
along with a blue fly –

signature of the universe
held in balance

by two tiny leaves
swaying in the breeze.

MIRACLE BOY

The all-weather pitch half-laid
is rich as a cinder path,
terrain to lift bars

into the air —
as if it were his own element,
and flight, second nature.

He's taught me to see
him defy gravity,
speak the lingo,

for where would life be
without tricks —
wheelies,

bunny hops, infinity rolls?
Despite falls
and wipe-outs,

clearing a ramp
or half-pipe, his passion
soars taking risks,

wheels riding thermals
in an open sky
like the boy

who ran free of the labyrinth
and flew too high.

LINES OF LATITUDE

Paris, Nice, Cairo.
I fell asleep over North Africa,
woke hours later,
without you, at the equator.
The plane rode turbulence –
like your plastic duck in water –

billowed into
the southern hemisphere.
Dawn over the Congo basin,
further than I'd ever been
from anywhere,
my eye followed

winding silver,
rainforest viridian,
pictured you sleeping
at home in bed with teddy
where it is
tomorrow morning.

EARTHWIRE

News came down the line,
your voice from home
a thousand miles from London,
calm, speaking of cancer.
Everything important up to then,
like who I loved or hated,
what show to see,
which dress to wear
or how my voice sounded in his ear,
froze into the March evening
shadows where I stood
with the black receiver
numb against my chin,
looking into darkness
and struggling to hold
your warm accented idiom,
saying who I was
and where I came from,
down to field and stream,
no matter how far I'd gone,
rooting me like lightning.

PANDORA'S BOX

Was this what Pandora sensed
as she looked at the box

she was asked to mind,
warned never to open

yet succumbed out of
curiosity, impishness,

the wish for importance?
The label says *printed matter*,

hardly volatile enough
to unleash the world's evil:

war, pestilence, famine.
For the time being

it rests in an outhouse,
beckoning as I pass.

Yet I keep my distance,
hedge my bets against Hope,

as if certain arrangements of
words could annihilate.

PRIMA DONNA

at Jennifer Johnston's
The Nightingale and Not the Lark

It was your face I saw
on stage last night,
the old woman sunk in her chair,
drink beside her on the floor,
hand an arc of
explanation in the air,

tears of bitterness and rage
with talk of roles played,
Juliet, Ophelia, Desdemona,
and the day he went
away as if it were
yesterday.

You I saw, bent
and wracked with sobs
at the memory of the plane
coming down and how
they found his body
with the other woman.

You, centre stage,
thank the house,
and now a flashback,
face lit, eyes smile,
young again,
the audience stand clapping.

CATHERINE OF ARAGON

When she undressed on the royal bed
under a canopy of silk, for one

who was husband and king,
lifting her gown of black satin

that flowed like water to receive him,
he saw that her flesh was burning.

She conceded how she'd come
to wear a hair shirt so that *God*

would take pity on her. He,
who from casement windows

glimpsed all the punishments
of court for treason – the rack,

cat-o'-nine-tails, even execution –
wept at how his own Cass,

his Spanish queen, was humbled
thus after fifteen years. Seeing

how she longed to carry his line,
he summoned to his palms

the coolness of linen as balm
to her skin when raising her

above him, and whatever
history might claim later,

it took no son to prove
their love was human.

THE SAFFRON DRESS

after Aeschylus

One day, hunting in the forest, the king
slaughtered a young deer, restless for war.
Winds dropped at Aulis and to Troy no fleet
could sail. For the price of fair wind
the goddess named Agamemnon's daughter,
Iphigenia, just come of age.

He sent for her, on pretext of marriage,
to his strong mountain palace, the king,
and told the queen to prepare her daughter
with talk of sons and husbands gone to war;
so women with fine needles in the wind
sewed a trousseau of silk, their hands fleet

while men at harbour deserted his fleet,
and that wife, in their private language,
voice in orange groves a summer wind,
sang a dream of love so clear, the king,
to settle old scores with Priam by war,
baulked at the rapture of his daughter,

who ran beside the carriage, daughter
of hilly Mycenae, agile and fleet
as a young deer, heedless of war,
under her breath, big name for his age,
'Achilles, Achilles', hero not king,
her joy lifting to the heavens like wind,

to the port, her passion a west wind
that stirred fresh doubt in her heart, daughter
in the wings, no one told her where her king
of hearts among warriors from the fleet
stood by the blazing fire that was the stage,
held by guards clearly decked for war,

and when she looked around in fear, war
almost come, a bride-to-be, for fair wind,
one met her eyes and saw her age
before the sacrifice, his daughter
for Troy above the flames, to bear the fleet
under full sail along with the pride of a king.

Winds shifted at the death of a daughter.
The fleet hoisted sails of a new war.
Love came to wage in the house of a king.

BROKEN DREAMS

You spoke of seeing that
trilogy. How Clytemnestra

mourning the sacrificed bride,
knelt on the ground,

hands cupping fresh soil,
face and arms smeared wild,

a mad woman howling
her betrayal to the skies.

In the silent fields round your house,
how invisible the griefs

that robbed you,
how unmarked your body,

and hidden the blood-flow.
By what goddess is your future

ransomed, what rough justice
taunts you across centuries?

And now that legendary scene
to confound your unsung life,

when the full brunt of the dark
that assaults you is milk.

INTO THE WEST

The yarn, live as fairytale –
time and again
you gazed transfixed and pale,
as if I wasn't there,

eyes wide and scared
as the eyes of the small boy
you lived through,
in trouble with the law,

crying for his mammy,
travel in his veins
reduced to asthma,
while he ran away

across the country
to the Atlantic coastline,
and our hero rode
into the ocean –

tense body
between my hands
poised like Oisín
carried by the sea.

LEAVETAKING

You would have me stare at a grave,
freshly dug, a precise rectangle,
though all around scattered in the grass
are primrose and daffodil,
folded petals beginning to open and frill.

You would have me stare at a grave,
spade marked, worms working the tilth,
though spring has come
after long winter, the blossoming plum
and at the doorstep earth's smell.

You would have me stare at a grave,
deeply cut, ready for burial,
though I am young and have known
love. If you must, bury yourself.
I will listen to the blackbird's trill.

THE OTHER SIDE

As if I were a corpse
and you were embalming me,
your hands trace
the contours of my face

with frankincense and bergamot,
my body insentient
to the warmth of your palms,
a coldness like knowledge

of something finally broken
is how it must be
at the end when Death comes.
The room so calm,

just me slipping away,
and on the other side
where it is still bright,
you performing

in the vast silence
of your attention
the last rite of my readiness
for transcendence.

THE GOLDFISH BOWL

The small glass tank sits outside
on the kitchen window ledge.
Already the water is viscous scum
tinted the stagnant green of ponds,

murky walls pocked with slime.
Single leaves have started to drift in.
Pollen. One of these days something
will start growing for the fish

to eat again. Pebbles on the bottom
have settled and filmed like a river bed.
The black cat waits motionless,
his eyes glued to two fish

at the far end, lying still,
one over the other, pretending not to
exist before his giant, whiskered head.
One morning they'll float

upside down, weightless as
rice-paper, or lie splayed
on the ledge, single specks of blood,
tiny bodies ripped to shreds.

INHERITANCE

The old house
abandoned now
looks in on itself,
thick limed walls,
slate roof an ample
haven for birds.
The floor, roughcast
stone and caked mud
is base for hay rake
and mow. Once
storm-proof,
simply furnished,
deep windows
define vision,
catch the sun.

GOING BACK HOME

The breeze blew open
the back door and gnawed timbers
gave way to sky,
grass in the yard.

I was chilled by a tunnel of air,
cold like light
coming from everywhere,
stars in the slates,
cracks in the wall.

This was supposed to be
summer, the sky
washed clean
for the third time that day,
the whole place tidy and bare
where once there was space
for everything:

Molly at the half-door
head dipped to water,
she drained as I watched
her nostrils flare,
daring to touch
the warm hairs,
after hoisting her collar
onto a nail, the wall
coming down with
things for hay – *súgán*,
pitchforks, rakes.

Even now, my limbs are
weighed with leather,
but the floor's so swept
and cleared, all that's left
is reduced to elements,

swallows' nests, cobwebs,
objects, hung with dust,
I don't recognise.

ACKNOWLEDGEMENTS

'*Fugit Amor*' and 'The First Rod: Mackerel at Inis Oírr' appeared in the *Irish Times*; 'Sparrow Thieves' appeared in *College English*; 'Seeds', 'Deluge', 'Island of Miracles' and 'The Freedom of the City' were published in *The Missouri Review*.

'Surfacing' is a translation of Eugenio Montale's poem '*A Galla*', from *Poesie Disperse, Tutte le Poesie* (Milan: Mondadori, 1984), which was commissioned by Marco Sonzogni for a collection of Montale's poetry in English.

Heartfelt thanks to the editors of *The Recorder: Journal of the Irish American Historical Society* for publishing '*Suantraí*', 'Origins', 'Mother Tongue', 'Going Back Home', 'Talking to God in a Protestant Church' and 'Gráinne's Bed', and to *The Canadian Journal of Irish Studies* for featuring my work, including: 'Paolo and Francesca', 'Wishing Tree in Cyprus', 'Fresh Tracks', 'Broken Dreams', 'Wonderstruck', 'Another Woman', 'The Big Freeze' and 'Earthwire'.

For first publication of poems in this book grateful acknowledgement is made to the following: *Agenda*, *At the Year's Turning* (Dublin: Dedalus, 1998), *Arabesque Review, The Art of Bicycling* (New York: Breakaway Books, 2005), *The Backyards of Heaven: An Anthology of Contemporary Poetry from Ireland and Newfoundland & Labrador* (2003), *The Clifden Anthology* (2002), *Cork Literary Review, New Hibernia Review, Poetry Daily, Poetry Ireland Review, Rhyme & Reason* (Dublin: Educational Company of Ireland, 2005), *The Shop, Something Beginning with P: New Poems from Irish Poets* (Dublin: O'Brien Press, 2004) and *The Southern Review*.

Thanks to the Australian poet Aileen Kelly for her reading of these poems, and her great wit and wisdom; to John Hobbs for his editorial advice; Niall MacMonagle for his support; and to my colleagues, Renate Ahrens, Sheila Barrett, Cecelia McGovern, Joan O'Neill and Julie Parsons for their friendship and support.

Finally, my thanks to Janice Smith and Patsy Horton at Blackstaff Press for their great care of the manuscript, and to my editor, Hilary Bell.